College Beloit

Exercises at the quarter-centennial anniversary of Beloit

College, July 9, 1872

College Beloit

Exercises at the quarter-centennial anniversary of Beloit College, July 9, 1872

ISBN/EAN: 9783337713461

Printed in Europe, USA, Canada, Australia, Japan

Cover: Foto ©ninafisch / pixelio.de

More available books at **www.hansebooks.com**

EXERCISES

AT THE

Quarter-Centennial

ANNIVERSARY

OF

BELOIT COLLEGE.

JULY 9, 1872.

~~~~~~~~~~~~~~~~~~~~~~~~~~~~~~~

BELOIT :

1872.

GARRET VEEDER, Printer, Janesville, Wis.

BELOIT COLLEGE

Quarter Centennial.

In anticipation of the Twenty-fifth Anniversary of Beloit College, the Board of Trustees, at their meeting in July 1871, appointed a committee consisting of the President, L. G. Fisher, Esq., Rev. G. S. F. Savage, D. D., and Rev. J. Collie, to make arrangements for the celebration of that event, the following year.

After conference with members of the Faculty and the Alumni, it was determined that the afternoon and evening of Tuesday, July 9th, 1872, should be occupied with the reading of several brief memorial papers on designated topics by representatives of the Trustees, the Faculty and the Alumni.

In accordance with this arrangement, in the afternoon of the day named, a goodly number of Alumni and other friends of the College gathered in the First Congregational Church. Rev. J. Collie, of the first class graduated, was called to the chair. The assembly joined in singing the doxology, "Praise God from whom all blessings flow." Rev. S. W. Eaton led in prayer. Then followed words of welcome from the President and the reading of the first six papers in order as here presented. The last two papers were read in the evening, after the Alumni Oration by Hon. C. W. Buckley of the class of 1860, and the Poem by Prof. P. Hendrickson of the class of 1867.

PRESIDENT CHAPIN'S

WORDS OF WELCOME.

I am charged with the pleasant duty on this happy anniversary, which closes the first quarter century of the life of Beloit College, to express her kindly greeting to her gathered sons and friends. Alumni of Beloit, each and all receive the glad welcome of Alma Mater, as you come back from your various homes and spheres of duty and care, to the family hearth-stone. You are here to honor this silver wedding-day, commemorative of her espousal to Christ, the King, in the interest of truth and right and sound learning, and the well-being of men, and the glory of God. She looks fondly on your manly faces. Her heart swells with worthy pride as she reviews the lives you have been living since you went out from her charge ; and she borrows the honors you have won, and wears them as jewels for her adornment to day. Your presence fills her heart with gladness and her face with smiles.

Be ye also glad. Make yourselves at home, as we sit down together to revive the associations of the past. Speak all your mind. As in sober conference we try to cast the future of the college, under the grave responsibility of a character and reputation already gained, give us the benefit of your observations in the world without, and speak to us words of cheer which shall animate our courage and inspire our endeavors to set this beloved institution forward for greater and better things, from this day forth. As you move again amid these classic halls and academic shades familiar to you all, know one another as brothers. Stand on no formalities of introduction, but let the common tie draw you freely and kindly to each other. So may you all both give and get a blessing from this festive assembling.

We include in this hearty welcome, not only the regular graduates, but all those who, in former years, have been for some time under instruction here, and whom the college loves to regard as her sons. We extend to you all a warm right-hand of greeting and a cordial invitation to this goodly fellowship, and we count as welcome friends also, all, whose interest in the general cause of education, as well as in this particular agency for it, has drawn them hither to-day.

Our arrangements are quite inadequate to fulfil all our desire. Our words must be few and hurried, but we trust they will bring up pleasant memories of the past, and present a bright and hopeful outlook for the future, and kindle in all our souls a fresh enthusiasm, and inspire prayers fervent and strong, to Him who has set the seal of his blessing on the college hitherto, and so prepare the way, under the continual guidance of divine wisdom and the help of divine power, for the life so auspiciously begun, to go on unfolding gracefully and grandly and more and more fruitfully to the end of the century, and on still on, for centuries to come. Now the seed that was planted here twenty-five years ago, was in its kind, like that of the California cedars, a germ of life for the centuries, nay more, it has bound up in it, the power of an endless life. The plant that sprung from it, though already fruitful, is yet in its infancy. Friends, brothers, sons, let it have your loving regard, your fostering care, your generous gifts, your prevailing prayers; for our aims and hopes for it are high and large.

A PAPER.

On the Acts and Aims of the Founders of Beloit College.

BY REV. A. L. CHAPIN, D. D.

PRESIDENT OF THE COLLEGE.

It devolves on me now, to begin these memorial exercises by presenting in pencil sketch, as well as I may, some of the initiatory steps taken for the founding of our college. The scene of the first sketch is in the old stone church of Beloit, in the Fall of 1843. The house was not quite finished, but when completed, a few weeks later, it stood the most stately and grand house of christian worship then in Wisconsin. It was at the time, made comfortable for the meeting of the General Presbyterian and Congregational Convention of Wisconsin, whose members, at that fall session, numbered just twenty-eight, representing all parts of the territory of Wisconsin, into which christian civilization had then made its way. It was my first introduction as a young pastor, to that body. I found those men then and there thinking on a college. They had been thinking on it for a year or more. Less than ten years after Black Hawk and his wild Indian troop had been chased by the Illinois volunteers under Lincoln and his compeers, up through this Rock River valley, those pioneers of Christ's army came in and had entertained the thought of planting a college, on the colony plan, away up by the beaver's dam on the head waters of this clear stream. They surmised correctly that the land could not be held in full posession by their king, till his power should be entrenched in such a stronghold of sanctified learning. They concluded to abandon that scheme, but the main thought was cherished still. A college must be built up and its life and strength must be the spirit of simple, self-sacrificing devotion to Christ's saving work. So much was clear and settled by that first step, from which they drew back.

Let me take you next, a few months later, in the early summer of 1844, to the door of a little state-room of the steamer Chesapeake, moving over the waters of Lake Erie and bearing as part of her freight, delegates returning from a great north-western gathering of christian men and women, that had been called at Cleaveland, to consider the general interests of Christ's kingdom in the wide Mississippi valley. You may see seven of us crowded together in that narrow room. Stephen Peet, to whom belongs the honor of being foremost and chief of the founders of Beloit College, is lying on the berth, ill in body, but his fertile mind as active as ever in planning for the spirit-ual interests of this region. By his side sits Theron Baldwin, then just entering on his life-work. Miter, Gaston, Hicks, Bulk-ley and myself are standing by, listening to their talk. The Western College Society was fairly organized and Baldwin, its Secretary and soul, unfolds its purpose and plans. There is light and hope in what he says. A hand from the East will be stretched out to help on the establishment of genuine christian colleges, judiciously located here and there in the West. Peet seizes on the gleam of encouragement, his uttered thoughts kindle enthusiasm and hope in the rest. There is an earnest consultation—there is a fervent prayer—there is a settled pur-pose and Beloit College is a living conception. The seven there, take on themselves the responsibility of calling a meeting of the friends of christian education in the three adjoining states of Illinois, Wisconsin and Iowa for definite consultation on the subject of providing institutions for liberal education under christian influences, in this part of the country. The steamer Chesapeake has long since gone to pieces, but of that conference on her deck came the framing of this good ship whose ribs and hull are wrought of eternal truths that know no decay, whose motive power is gendered by the fire of Christ's love turning into vital forces irrepressible, the latent energies of human souls, whose course is laid to run for the ages, till all the ends of the earth shall see the salvation of our God.

It was the 6th of August, 1844, when the meeting convened in the same old stone church, of sacred memory. From Iowa came four, from Illinois twenty-seven, from Wisconsin twenty five—fifty-six in all. The honest, brave and good brother Kent, was called to preside. For two days they talked and prayed over the question before them, in a frank, earnest, independent spirit, with some sharp collision of opinions but with harmonious results. They decided that a college ought immediately to be established in Iowa, and that the exigences of northern Illinois and Wisconsin required a college and a female Seminary of the highest order to be established, each near the border line. A committee of ten was appointed to consider the action necessary to carry out the purpose and report to a future convention. The second convention met in October of the same year and was composed of fifty members, all from Wisconsin and Illinois. They reaffirmed the previous decision, but know-ing that the success of the enterprise must depend on the hearty co-operation of the churches, definite action was still deferred and measures were taken, through circulars and committees of visitation, to give information and awaken interest more gener-ally on the subject. A third convention, the largest of all, numbering sixty-eight, assembled in May, 1845, and after ear-nest and prayerful discussion, reviewing the whole subject, with only one dissenting voice, located the college in Beloit. The plans for the Female Seminary could not then be matured. In October 1845, a fourth convention met and adopted a form of charter and elected a Board of Trustees for the College, and so the ship was launched.

The first meeting of the Board of Trustees can never be for-gotten by those present. It was held October 23d, 1845, in the basement of the old church, immediately after the last con-vention adjourned. Eight of the fifteen were there, Kent and Peet and Hickcox, whose work on earth is now done, and Clary and Pearson and Fisher and Talcott and Chapin, still mem-bers of the Board. They sat in silence for a while, looking in each other's faces and trying to realize the responsibilities of the trust imposed upon them. One said, at last, "Well, breth-ren, what are we to do?" The ready answer came from brother Kent, "*Let us pray.*" The prayer that then went up to heaven, warm and fervent from his lips, carrying the hearts of all, was the first gasp of the new-born college for life. The breath of a divine inspiration, we believe, came upon it then, and its history since, has been the continued answer to that prayer.

One more date and one more scene demand notice in this record of first steps. It was the 24th of June, 1845, "The day,—a great day for Beloit and its infant college—was as bright as ever dawned, and never did the green slopes of broad prairies spread themselves in greater beauty to the eye of men anywhere, than as seen that day from the college bluff." So opens the newspaper report at the time. The people of the village, and hundreds from the neighboring towns, and some from remote parts of the land, were marshaled in formal procession under the direction of our honored and lamented fellow citizen, John M. Keep, Esq., and proceeded to the chosen site. There, an assembly estimated to number nearly two thousand was gathered in the open air. Passages of Scripture were read by Rev. M. Montague; a reverend brother from Connecticut offered prayer, a choir of sweet voices made the grove resound to the praise of God, as they sung one of David's psalms. A historical sketch, (for the college had a history even then) was read by your present speaker, and Rev. Mr. Peet stated that resources secured for the enterprise, were the choice site of ten acres on which they stood and a building begun by the citizens of Beloit in fulfillment of their pledge ; a gift of 160 acres in Milwaukee County from an Eastern friend, and lands valued at $10,000.00, donated by the Hon. T. W. Williams of Connecticut as a foundation for the first professorship. There, in place of one formal extended discourse expected from Prof. Stowe, whom illness prevented from fulfilling his appointment, the hour was filled up by brief, off-hand, pointed speeches from some of our Western men called suddenly to meet the emergency. First came our giant brother Montgomery, whose great body and great soul were all aglow with enthusiasm as he argued that Western minds should be educated on Western soil and that the education of the West should be *expanded, liberal* and *democratic,* a *universally polished Westernism.* Next, Rev. T. M. Hopkins, of Racine, with pointed and forceful words set forth the importance of training mind to *independent thinking* and the advantages for doing this here in the far West. Then, Rev. F. Bascom, an early pioneer in this field, met the practical question, "*cui bono?*" " why so much expense

on education?" by a clear and impressive presentation of the
dependence of the practical arts on the researches of science
and the important influences which emanate from a true christian
college for the general intelligence and the moral purity and
health of the whole community. He was followed by Rev.
S. G. Spees, then of Cincinnati, whose imagination, kindled by
the scene, saw in the burr-oak openings of the bluff a veritable
grove of Parnassus, and in the clear water of Rock River, a
stream as good for inspiration as that which flowed from Cas-
talia's fount; and out of these classic allusions in connection
with the occasion, he drew some good common sense
reasons for making the education imparted here, *thorough*.
Then all passed to the rising walls near by, and after a few
plain, fit words, Rev. Mr. Kent, the President of the Board, laid
in due form the corner-stone of the first building, and in fervent
prayer, consecrated anew the whole enterprise to Christ and
the service of his Kingdom. Thus Beloit College gained a
local habitation as well as a name. It was a good day of
blessed influences. Little boys who watched with childish curi-
osity the proceedings, caught there the impulse which, in due
time, brought them under the culture of the college. The faith
of the community in the ultimate success of the enterprise was
strengthened. New friends were enlisted. The hearts of the
trustees were encouraged and from this literal *commencement*,
the College started forward at once, for its legitimate work.

I can linger no longer on these early scenes, nor will I
attempt an elaborate exposition of the *aims* contemplated by
those who thus laid the foundations. They are sufficiently
indicated by the sketches I have given. In these early coun-
sels, representatives of the Congregational and Presbyterian
churches, then in the region, mingled in about equal propor
tions. They came together not with any sectarian zeal, but
as christian men, joined in heart and hand for a great and good
work. They regarded a *positive, religious influence* as essential to the completeness of a liberal education, and their aim was
defined to be, to make this college in all its teaching and influence, not narrowly denominational but broadly and purely and
positively evangelical,. They were swayed by no personal, no
local or sectional interests, but by thoughtful consideration on

the needs of human society and the grand purpose of Gods, redeeming providence and the obligation resting on all men of christian culture to help on the civilization of the world and its subjection to the Lord, Christ. Their aim was to establish an institution to which young men from any part of the land or of the world might come and prepare themselves to go out into all parts of the world and labor for the well-being of men and the glory of God. It was made a condition of the first donation received from abroad, that the college should know no distinction of race and color. The condition was heartily accepted; for it was in full accord with the thought and aims of the founders. On the roll of students are found representatives of the Anglo-Saxon, the Keltic, the Kymric, the Gailic, the Teutonic, the African, the aboriginal American, the Armenian, and the Japanese races; and the sons of the college are already abroad laboring for the advancement of nearly all these races on their native soil.

And for its interior work, the detailed processes of culture, the aim distinctly contemplated from the beginning is to make thorough work with young men in the training part of a liberal, christian education. The course of study prescribed aims at a systematic, widely varied and precise drilling of all the powers of the mind, by exercise in the leading departments of human thought and learning. The end sought is a symmetrical developement of all the faculties in a way to give the man full command of those faculties for any purpose, and christian elements are made to pervade the whole process, that the relation of religious truth to all other forms of truth may be apprehended and that the perfect balance of the man in character may be secured by the combined culture of mind and heart.

In the earnest prosecution of their aims, Beloit College has been thus far administered and God has blessed it. For the future, we ask only more wisdom, more steadiness of purpose more whole-souled consecration to the same high aims.

A PAPER:

On the Relation of Beloit College to the People of Beloit and Its Vicinity,

BY REV. D. CLARY,

Secretary of the Board of Trustees, from the Beginning.

and I really wish that I had more time and ability to do it full

To me and to many others this is a topic of great interest, justice.

This relation might be contemplated in various particulars, the secular or financial, the legal, the ecclesiastical, the social, educational, as well as the moral and religious; but my remarks will be confined, mainly, to the last, viz.: *The moral and religious.*

Those of us who are well acquainted with this whole subject, can easily trace the relation, in all its aspects, to the early settlement of the place, just as those who are well informed respecting the origin of the free institutions of our country, can trace it to the early settlers of this country who first " placed their feet on the wild New England shore."

Those institutions political and religious and their concomitants existed in embryo in the principles and purposes which brought them here; and we to-day, with *all* the people, yes, (blessed be the God of our fathers,) *all the* people of all complexions and all nationalities, enjoy the two hundred and more years developement of those principles and those purposes.

So when a colony of christian families and christian individuals, in 1837, from New England, located at Beloit, they had it in their hearts to establish the institutions of religion and religious education, and here, while most of them lived in shanties and unfinished houses, they built a house for schools, for religious meetings and for such other purposes as might be for the best interests of the people. In that house the common schools and religious meetings were, at once, established.

As soon as practicable (1842) they commenced to build a house of worship. It was one of the first three in Wisconsin. In the meantime a charter for an academy was obtained, and as soon as the basement was sufficiently finished, the academy was in operation there.

In August, 1844, a convention of christian ministers and laymen from the churches of Wisconsin and Northern Illinois, was held in the first Congregational church, to consider the subject of establishing a college. Trustees were appointed and Beloit was selected as the most eligible location, and the citizens, true to their moral and religious principles, made the most liberal offer of means for the work, accompanied by a pledge of continued aid and especially of earnest prayer for God's blessing on the enterprise.

Already in the first laying out of the town plot, had the street running North and South on the East side of the present college site been named by a kind of prophetic instinct, College Street.

Thus came into being this collegiate offspring of the early settlers of Beloit, and when a college class was formed of five young gentlemen, it was placed under the instruction of the Principal of the academy. (And I shall be pardoned, I am sure, for saying here, that it was our esteemed friend and fellow citizen Mr. S. T. Merrill.)

Here we may see the origin of the relation of Beloit College to Beloit people.

And with the growth of the college, and its progress toward maturity, the reasons have multiplied for regarding the relation as one of great importance, one of mutual responsibility and interest. *On the part of the college,* we have the moral and religious influence of a large number of Professors and teachers, all of them christians, and most of them ministers of the Gospel. This influence, besides being given to the two hundred students under their care, one-fifth of whom are from Beloit, is felt in the place, generally, and in all departments of society. The same is true, in measure, of the large number of earnest christian students, with respect to their fellow students, and others also.

By them, for the most part, have been gathered and sustained, for many years past the twelve or fifteen sabbath schools in the near vicinity of the place. Morever, through the influence of the college, many families are led to seek a residence here for the purposes of education, and to enjoy the society.

And with reference to other schools from the primary upward. it appears to me that all right minded persons see and feel that not only is there no conflict of interests between them and the college but that their interests are all in one direction, viz. that of thorough education under healthful moral influence, and therefore, that a true friend to one will be a true friend to all.

Thus much, and from necessity in brief, on the part of the college ; and on the part of the people is it more than reasonable to expect that they will aim to throw around the college their influence for good? Is not this included in the pledge given at the outset? 'Tis true that but very few of us were there to unite in the pledge, nor were we present in that old Hall in Philadelphia when the "life, fortune and sacred honor" of the thirteen American colonies (by their representatives) were pledged to make this a free country, but what friend to his country refuses to come under that pledge? With it are handed down the blessings. So the pledge and the benefits of this college to this people, have come down together to us.

It was, in a great degree, owing to the fact that there was a large number of christian families in the place that the college was located here. Beloit was complimented, not long since, by a leading christian gentleman of Milwaukee when he said that "Beloit was the only place then in Wisconsin, where there was religion enough to have a college."

This was intended in the true sense to be a *christian* college, a school where the morals of the students might have special care, and where those who desired it might be aided in prepar ing for the ministry. Hence the original plan of the Founders was to have the students board in families so that they might be under the daily influence of christian *homes!* and that plan was not given up while families in a sufficient number were open to them, and at such expense as they could afford to meet.

In a company of two hundred (less or more) young men, not all of them yet attained to manhood, is it not reasonable to expect much difficulty in keeping them all, and always, under perfect control ? Despite the *best*, the *wisest* and most *judicious* efforts on the part of their instructors, irregularities amounting some terms to *outbreaks* were to be expected. It is the experience of the oldest colleges in the land, and while it is fair to attribute these, oftentimes, to impetuosity and vicious proclivities of some students, can it be truthfully denied that these things are often traced and traceable to demoralizing influences in the community? and is it uncharitable to believe that if there were no intoxicating liquors sold, and no other places where vice is nurtured, there would be less evils of the kind alluded to? At any rate it appears to me that the experiment is well worth a fair trial.

But to the churches, the professedly religious portion of this people, the college looks for support in this direction, and to christian churches of all denominations this appeal ought to be confidently made.

The college is neither an ecclesiastical nor a sectarian institution. Students, in coming to it, are not questioned as to their denominational preferences, except so far as may help them to decide where they choose to attend church services. *That choice* once made, they are encouraged to pay due attention to the service chosen, but in all respects, the utmost religious freedom is enjoyed.

But I have already gone beyond the ten or twelve minutes of time allotted. I must close in few words. While calling, as I have done, on the people of Beloit, irrespective of creed or denominational relations, to give their moral and religious influence to the college, I readily offer, in behalf of the college, the assurance that it has been the steady aim of its conductors in time past to promote the best interests of the people, and I have the fullest confidence that such will its aim be in the future,—and may we not all unite in the hope and expectation that, by the united exertions and earnest prayers of both the college and the people, it will be, for long years, even ages to come, a blessing to the people here, and far away, to all people and all nations on the Earth.

A PAPER:

On the Inner Life of the College.

BY REV. J. COLLIE.

Class of 1851.

Life still remains an occult force which eludes analysis, a "burning bush" beyond which the Creator does not permit scientific investigation to approach Him.

A consideration of what we figuratively call the "inner life" of a college, leads to deal with its most fundamental facts and touches the roots of all its external relations.

Every college has a life, a spirit, a distinct form, yet breathing through its government, its course of scholastic and scientific study and the intercourse of the members of its community and it is a far more vital question, what that spirit is, than, what are the institution's facilities for mental discipline, for unless the spirit is right the training afforded must be inadequate and wrong.

It is this "life" of the college which settles what shall be the *end* at which students will aim and toward which they will practically work. By this the character and measure of *enthusiasm*, in the pursuit of learning, will be decided. It is this which will determine whether the training imparted shall lay hold of *every department* of the immortal nature or whether it shall ignore the broadest and most central part, and thus be partial, unbalanced, and in some respects, positively injurious.

This "life" may be of very dissimilar character. Each institution has its own peculiar tone. The limited time assigned to this paper permits to glance only at the general spirit of a Christian College and then to attempt a comparision with what we shall find that to be, of the actual life of this honored Institution, the young mother of some two hundred sons.

The difference between a Christian and a non-Christian education, is not one of modes of instruction, of courses of study, of arts and sciences taught, but a difference of underlying principles, of aim and spirit. The two are more widely diverse than the Ptolemaic and Copernican theories in Astronomy, for these disagree as to whether one finite object or another is the center of the solar system, while those differ on the question whether an infinite or a finite being, God or man, shall be the final end of education.

The real life of a Christian college does not lie in an earnest defence and inculcation of the distinctive truth of revelation, nor in the regular observance of the worship of God, nor even in cultivating the spiritual capabilities of its students. However important all these may be, it does not by itself afford the *vitality* we seek. In order to secure that, we must begin with the recognition of the fact that *all true education proceeds from God*, and *must* do so in order to lead to Him. That it is not something calculated to His Kingdom, being adjacent, yet not of it, but one of that Kingdom's central forces, a power that is kindred to God's creative energy, for it builds up the whole being in the fair proportions of the divine ideal. We must accept it as a part of His redemptive work in that it sets a supremely worthy object of life and culture before the student and gathers about him the most pure and potent incentives to its attainment, thus lifting him to a broader and worthier life.

A Christian college then is a Fountain in which *God*, with the gracious forethought of a Father for the want of his children, has stored those facilities and influences needful to a comprehensive culture of mind and heart. If we admit that coal-beds and springs of water, testify to the providential care of God for the physical wants of man, surely the human agency employed in building up institutions for invigorating and purifying immortal minds, does not warrant us in denying that they too are ordained of God.

If then a College is to be Christian in spirit as well as in name, its Faculty and Board of trust need first of all, to put themselves into vital contact with Him who is the Light and the Life of the world, that through them the college may root itself in God, and being persuaded that their institution is from God, they need to be firm in the purpose that it shall be *for* Him, and this persuasion must be so deep and this purpose so earnest that they shall be willing to venture the expenditure of their own life and the success of their undertaking upon them.

The sentiment that all true culture is of God and for God, must glow in their life and be carried over with impressive power to the minds of those whom they are treating.

And if this is to be done; if divine energy and blessing conveyed by the college are to penetrate the life of its students, if the college is to be a cosmos of noble aims, of clearer light and worthier enthusiasm, if the instructors would wield the full force of personal influence, so potent to stimulate and guide the young, then they must not only be in vital connection with Christ, but they must also win the hearts of the students. In order to the highest results of even mental dicipline, the teacher needs the hearts of his pupils, much more than to give that harmonious training of mind and spirit which it is the province of the Christian college to impart.

These sentiments are expressed with the greater confidence because they correspond so nearly with those which have produced the actual history of this institution.

Beloit College is one of God's facts. He foreordained it. He inspired those prayer-cries in the midst of which it had its birth. His grace which quickens and purifies both intellect and spirit has been its life. He awakened that prophet's voice in the hearts of the early settlers of this region which gave them no rest, till, from far over the prairies they met and covenanted to prepare the way of the Lord as He came with the blessings of learning and Heavenly wisdom to enrich and adorn the youth of coming generations.

He wrought that self consecration in the noble men who, in its early days, identified themselves with it when, as yet, it was but a vision seen by the eye of faith.

From him came that courageous, persistent, self denying spirit by which, through these years of wearing, poorly appreciated labor, those men and others who have become associated

with them, have worked on, "by faith" "preparing" a college
"to the saving" of the people. As doing His bidding they
have been launching young men on that stream of Christian
culture which flows forever toward God, and blesses the world
through which it flows. Here the aim has been to present an
object of life not connected with an order of things which is
destined to vanish away, and which is ever crumbling under
our touch, but with an order, substantial and eternal. For why
should a soul train and develope itself, when as a matter of fact
it knows of no aim of life which, in the sober hour, is not felt
to be a shadow and a sorrow. Or in other words the aim has
been that the student might know himself, not only as a thinker
and a man of science, but as God's prophet, having cognizance
of things unseen as well as those visible to reason and sense.—
To hear and utter the voice of God within him as well as to
read the writing on the walls of the temple of science.

From the earliest days of Beloit its students have found mingled with the very atmosphere of this hill the sentiment that,
Faith in God, and Faith in the nature which God has given us,
is necessary to the right understanding of the things, that are
seen, and they have been fortunate enough, here to be brought
under the influence of personal character which is a practical
embodiment and commendation of that Faith.

Amid the dissolving confidence of men in everything which
they themselves have not devised, which so largely characteri-
zes this generation, those who have been intrusted with the
administration of this institution have, while "keeping abreast
of the times" retained their faith in the distinctive idea of the
American Christian College, an institution which specially
makes room for the presence and power of God in the unfolding
and molding of the minds which He has created. This faith
shaped the policy of the college from the first, as is indicated by
the pledge of its first President,—happily its President to-day—
made at his inauguration twenty-two years ago, to give his
"undivided energies to the building up of this college for the
service and glory of Him who is head over all," and that the
institution has not swerved from its early faith and purpose, in
this respect, is emphatically declared by the same writer in a

recent article, from which we quote, "to give the balance of complete developement the praise of noblest manhood, Chris-tian truth and morality need to be infused through all the educational process."

The indwelling life of the college has taken on a practical embodiment in various ways. Members of the first class within a year of its formation, organized and conducted two Sunday schools in neighboring communities, not enjoying the privileges of the sanctuary. By the third year, four such schools were formed and the number has been increased in late years, and on some of them the renewing grace of God has been richly bestowed.

But little more than two years of the college's existence had passed, when the present Missionary Society was organized for the twofold purpose of inquiring into the state and claims of the work in the foreign field and for maintaining neighborhood meetings and Sunday Schools in the vicinity of Beloit.

As one of the results of a marked revival in the college a few years since the college prayer meeting which had been kept up from the earliest years of the institution, became a daily meeting which is still maintained, and this "inner life" which has been rising higher and becoming more full from time to time, in the history of the college, has been as heaven among the favored youth who have been gathered here. That life which is not capable of imparting itself is not of the highest type. Beloit College has imparted her spirit to her sons.

Here the inspiration has been caught which has made young hearts valiant to struggle and die for their country and humanity, and on this glad anniversary yon "Memorial Hall" carries our minds back to the grand years of conflict for national existence, back to the grim or somber scenes amid which more than forty young men from Beloit College laid down their lives for the Republic.

Here that devotion to Christ has been kindled which has borne some select spirits to the ends of the earth to carry to the dying souls of men some measure of that "life" by which their Alma Mater nourished them.

And so this "inner life" has broken forth, to pour itself in

streams of manifest blessing along this and succeeding ages.—
Our ears have heard the first gurgling of this outbursting life
as it leaps from the fountain, and we believe that we shall see
that stream grow broad and deep, sparkling in the light of that
day when the New Jerusalem shall descend from heaven. We
expect to hear the murmur of its flowing, blending with the
hosannas of a world redeemed, when the life of Christ poured
out upon the world and over the world, shall have made all
things new.

A PAPER:

Reminiscences of Early Days and the Financial Affairs of the College.

BY PROFESSOR J. J. BUSHNELL.

There is perhaps, a kind of classic, Homeric propriety, in assigning to the oldest among the co-laborers here, the office of story teller,—and there is a pleasant suggestion too, of modern Yankee caution, in sandwiching the story in between the two ends of fifteen minutes. I heartily accept the situation, however, in both its aspects and, as these reminiscences are to be personal, I shall be pardoned if they deal much with the first person, singular number and nominative case.

On the 27th of April, 1848, I came in sight of Beloit, as the lumbering vehicle called Frink & Walker's stage, rose over the crest of the hill to the northeast of Roscoe. As we descended the hill and drove through the street of that village, I saw, for the first time, I think, this side of Cleveland, a dry street and solid road bed of mingled gravel and sand, and my ear was greeted with the unusual sound of pebbles grinding under the coach wheels. I shouted at once to the driver, "Is Beloit anything like this? Do they have gravel there?" "Yes, just like this," was the answer. "Ah! that is the place for a college, then," said I to myself.

My enthusiasm for gravel will be understood from the fact that for five years I had been connected with a college in Ohio, confessedly first in the West at that time, but which was located in a region of pure clay; rough and hard to the feet as rock under the summer sun, giving an unknown depth of mud in the winter and early spring, and slippery as soft soap in the drizzles of spring and autumn; and the crisp sound of the gravel under the wheels was pleasantly suggestive of dry walking, and clean boots, and pleasant excursions on Wednesday and Saturday af-

ternoons, and all that free out door air and exercise which is so
conducive to the healthy life of a college; and there is no doubt,
I think, that the dry gravel streets, and pleasant walks over the
firm soil and gravel bluffs in this vicinity, did much to give Beloit
its early popularity as a place for educational institutions. It is in
these respects without equal among the small cities of the Northwest.

I landed from the stage at the old Rock River House, late in
the afternoon of April 27, 1848, and soon found my way to the
house of Rev. Mr. Clary, then, as now, the Secretary of the
Board of Trustees. The invitation which had brought me hither was, to come and assist in the preliminary steps for the organ-
ization of the college. I knew nothing of what had been done;
and the first thing therefore was, to know the ground, the means
to work, and the community to work for and upon.

It will perhaps be a marvel to the future historian, that Beloit
College began to be a college upon such slender means, and upon so narrow a pecuniary basis. A few inquiries brought out the
facts, that at the time of my arrival the College had no cash funds;
that its only resources were a donation of lands from Maj. Thos.
W. Williams, of New London, Conn., from which it was expected that $10,000 would be realized, and another small tract of land,
sold soon after for $1,000. Besides these, the city of Beloit had
pledged a site, and the erection of the first building, and two
years before they had raised for the building a subscription of
$7,000, and given a site of ten acres. Disaffection to the enter-
prise, had crept in, on the question of slavery or anti-slavery, and
the subscription of $7,000 had dwindled to $5,000. Of this subscription, $4,000 had been collected and expended in the summer
of 1847, in putting up the bare brick walls of Middle college; and
the remainder, $1,000, was not available, as it was subscribed in
labor in some form, which could not be used without money to
put with it. For six months preceding my arrival, the walls of
Middle College had stood floorless, windowless and roofless, without any available means to finish it.

Still behind this enterprise, thus weak as it seemed, stood the
pledge of the Congregationalists and New School Presbyterians
of the region northwest of Chicago and east of the Mississippi

River, unanimously expressed in several large conventions, to unite in building, at Beloit, one strong institution, thus avoiding the error, so fatal elsewhere, of wasting their energies and means upon a number of rival or abortive projects.

But slender and inadequate as the means of the College were, it had already made a beginning. Five young men had been fitted for college in Beloit Seminary, under the instruction of Mr. S. T. Merrill, and were organized into a Freshman class in 1847, and continued under the charge of Mr. Merrill for the greater part of the Freshman year. This was the beginning of Beloit College. Mr. Merrill filled worthily, that year, the positions of President and Professor, in all departments. Early in May, 1848, Mr. Merrill transferred the instruction of this first class to me, and it remained in my hands a few weeks, till the approaching meeting of the Board of Trustees. On the 23d of May, 1848, Prof. Emerson reached Beloit, on the same errand which had brought myself hither four weeks before. He came directly to my room, and almost his first question was, "Can we have a college here?" Having had some experience in building up a college in Ohio, already twenty years old, and still in peril of failure, and a vivid consciousness of our meager resources, I answered, "Yes—if we will make it." How heartily my honored colleague accepted this view, and set himself to the work of *making* a college here, may be understood from the fact that more than $50,000 of the present funds of the College have come to us through the voluntary, constant and watchful influence of the Emerson family.

On the next day, the 24th of May, 1848, was the meeting of the Board of Trustees. After assigning to Mr. Emerson the department of languages, and to myself that of mathematics, the pressing question of the time came up,—How can the college building be finished? It had become apparent that very considerable disaffection to the enterprise had been developed by jealousies and party feeling, even in Beloit, that the friends of the College here were somewhat discouraged, and felt that they had done all they could ; and the weather beaten brick walls seemed to tell of a community that began to build, and were unable to finish. Still, the answer to the inquiry came back from the Trustees resident abroad, and from the new Professors: Beloit must fulfill its pledge, and build the first building. To this it was answered that Beloit had virtually redeemed its pledge, for the site at first contemplated, at the south end of Mr. Rood's farm, could have been bought for $500, and the site selected was worth $3,000. What Beloit had failed to give in a building, it had made up in giving a more eligible and expensive site. To this it was answered still, that Beloit was pledged before the world to give the site and the first building; that it was useless to go abroad for funds till that pledge was redeemed, and that a new subscription in Beloit of at least $2,000 was absolutely necessary. The Trustees resident here knew well the discouraged state of feeling, and were with reason somewhat faithless of success, but consented that the new professors, somewhat sanguine and self-confident young men, should undertake the work. One of them therefore, took upon himself the work of instruction of the college class, and the other, under the guidance of the well remembered Deacon Hinman, the most polite and pleasant gentleman in Beloit of that time, commenced a thorough canvass of the city, man by man, not to solicit subscriptions, but to talk College. This was followed up for three weeks, till almost every man had been seen personally. Much of indifference, some opposition to an abolition college, and still more of discouragement, were at first encountered, but as the visitors went on, from day to day, it was soon apparent that the ice was broken : that some feeling, some curiosity, some hope were excited. The tide began to rise, and by the latter part of June the way seemed to be prepared for a public meeting. The appointment was made, and the same method was pursued, of inviting all to the meeting, man by man.

Of course some planning was necessary to make the meeting successful, but so fearful were the resident Trustees that the people of Beloit would feel that the matter was crowded upon them, or that some "snap game" was "being come over" them, that they refused to have any arrangements made to take advantage of any rising excitement of the meeting, or ask for any subscriptions on the spot. It was decided that two resolutions should be offered, the first declaring that it was expedient that Beloit should raise $2,000 more to complete the College building; the second, that a committee should be appointed to solicit subscriptions for that purpose.

The meeting came. The fruits of three weeks' canvassing were visible in a house well filled with the best and ablest citizens. The young Professors made their maiden speeches in Beloit. Mr. Hazen Cheney, in his timid, hesitating manner, moved the first resolution, but followed it up with about one minute of most effective speaking. He reminded the chairman that in subscribing $150 two years before, he gave at that time all he was worth; but rather than have the enterprise fail, "I am ready," said he, with emphasis, "to give another hundred dollars." Good Deacon Hobart, not being versed in the proper order of spontaneous movements in public meetings, here rose to offer the second resolution. The Chairman gently reminded him that his time was not yet. The short speech of Mr. Cheney seemed to touch the right chord, and his resolution was adopted by acclamation. The Deacon then arose. All present knew that that large hearted man, in subscribing $400 before, had given to the College a large percentage of his property. After stating his motion, he remarked that he supposed every one present would feel that he had done all that could be expected of him; but still, rather than see a failure in this matter, if it were necessary to raise the sum required, he might be counted upon for another hundred dollars. A third person immediately arose and pledged another $100. The Chairman, Deacon Hinman, was the man for the occasion. "Gentlemen," said he, "we must not pass these things by. We must have a secretary, and take down these pledges, and then let this beginning be followed by short, pithy speeches, of like character, from all quarters. Let everybody be free to speak, and speak to the point." The hint was taken. Persons rose successively in all parts of the house, pledging $100, $75, $50 and $25. Mr. S. C. Field rose and said that he had no money, but he would give 160 acres of land. It proved the most important subscription of the evening, and was sold almost immediately for $400 in cash. The volunteer subscriptions of that evening to raise the sum of $2,000, footed up about $2,400, and a thorough canvass of the village soon carried the subscription up to $4,000.

But though the sum necessary for finishing the building had been subscribed, it was not yet paid. The following winter and spring of '48-9 was a time of scarcity of money, of which the last two years, hard as we think they are, give us no conception. Wheat was about three shillings a bushel, and dressed pork on the street 1¾ cents per pound. The work of finishing the building went slowly and heavily on, and the workmen were paid chiefly in orders on the stores. Except the $400 paid from the land given by Mr. Field, scarcely $300 was collected in cash from the whole subscription; the remainder was paid by orders, labor, and in every way which the ingenuity of the building agent could devise, and in this expensive and tedious way the building finally absorbed nearly the whole $4,000.

In some of the emergencies incident to the erection of the building, the sum of $800 in cash, derived from the sale of Major Williams' lands, and sacred to invested funds had been used and gone into the building. In more euphonious language, the building fund was debtor to the invested fund $800. It was very evident that no such sum could be collected from the remnant of the subscriptions for the building, for a large share of them was payable only in labor or materials. Still, honesty to Major Williams, the donor, required that his fund should be made good. In this emergency, the bright idea struck the inquiring mind of the building agent, that he might build these subscriptions of labor and materials into a dwelling-house which would be soon called for by the increasing population; sell it and from the proceeds replace the malappropriated funds. The lot directly south of the college grounds was at once purchased, I think for fifty dollars, and the house now well known as the Hinman house was put forward immediately. Boys were employed to gather the cobble stones from the bed of Turtle Creek, all the broken brick about the college building were economized to fill in behind the facework, and all labor which could be procured upon the subscription was made available. Into that building was built with his own hands a subscription of $100, from our old friend and citizen, Alex. Douglass. There Mr. Chester Clark, one of the large family of Clark brothers then resident here, worked out his subscription in laying the cobble stone walls, employing therefor chiefly the skillful masonry of the editor of "the Stumbling Stone." There the Messrs. Gates, who are gone from us now, left an enduring memorial in the substantial cut stones which build up the corners of the building. About $800 of subscriptions were thus worked into the building; it cost with the ground $1475,—was sold for all it cost, and a sunken college fund was replaced,—a thing, so far as I know, not happening before or since. Would that we might see such a phenomenon again in regard to the Memorial building.

The lapse of my appointed time admonishes that this rather minute narrative should come to a close. I have limited myself to the financial matters of the first year of my connection with the college, because, although these transactions concerned but trifling sums and small matters, compared with the ten thousands and one hundred thousands subscribed for eastern colleges at the present day, yet they were important to us. It has always seemed to me, that if there has ever been a crisis in the history of this college, it was at the time when Beloit raised her second subscrip- tion of $4000, and the success with which that effort was carried through, inspired courage and hope through all the time thereafter.

I cannot close this narrative, however, without briefly alluding to one thing more in which the financial events of the years '48 and '49 culminated, settling the question of permanency of the college, and making '48 to '50 the most successful period in that respect, of our history. During these years, Mrs. S. W. Hale, of Newburyport, Mass., a lady of large, liberal heart, and possessed of resources which had already been felt in the building of Andover Theological Seminary, and in every form of Christian benevolence, had her attention directed to the needs of our infant institution.

As the result, Prof. Emerson placed in my hands the United States patents for 5,000 acres of lands in Coles county, in eastern Illinois, as the donation of Mrs. Hale. The college has received and invested from them about $35,000.

And now in closing, permit us to record, with devout uprising of heart to God, that the early instructors in this college were not at any time called to endure those privations,—and harrassings of debt,—and heart soreness of hopes deferred, which have enter- ed into the early history of some Western Colleges. From the outset, the salaries, though small, have been promptly paid, and were sufficient for their present necessities, and the early work of the college though laborious, was not trying. Under God's fa- vor it was carried forward, with an elasticity of feeling, a buoy- ancy of hope, a confidence of expectation, which made all labors

easy and every burden light.   It was for us a harvest work from
the beginning, calling for faithful labor, but yielding its rewards
abundantly.   Privations and sacrifices indeed there were, some
on our part, and much also on the part of others, whose names
are held in grateful remembrance.   Among these we recall as
worthy of special honor those generous home missionaries, who
set apart from their small inadequate salaries, one hundred dollars each, to found Beloit College.   To such belong the dignity
and blessing of sacrifices,—ours was the pleasant lot and privilege
of joyous and successful work.

[Note.—Peter McVicar, D. D., of the class of 1856, President of Washburn College, Kansas, was requested to prepare a paper on the relation of the college to Christian education. As his engagements have ever forbade his meeting the request, President J. W. Strong consented to speak on this topic, in connection with that assigned to him.]

A PAPER:

On the Relation of the College to the Church and Kingdom of Christ; and to Education.

BY REV. J. W. STRONG, D. D.

Class of 1858. *President of Carleton College.*

A full discussion of these two broad themes is not now necessary. The fitness of that culture which the Christian college secures, for the work of evangelizing the world has been in constant demonstration in this land, ever since our fathers founded the first New England college, as its motto declared, "*Christo et ecclesiæ.*" I cannot speak of this culture as exemplified here, without involving ideas fundamental to our whole American civilization. It is a chief glory of that civilization that it began in the religious instincts of man,—in the better part of our nature, —and so it was not, nor has it ever been, narrow and selfish, but, instead, broad and Christian in its aim; touching at every point, the church and kingdom of Christ, involving individual liberty and social elevation, and therefore, noble and far-reaching in its results. To-day and here, are the fruits of that religious impulse manifest,—for New England is the real mother of us all, and whether we look at our political theories, our educational systems, or our religious principles, we easily trace the features of the mother's face. This likeness in character and in aim, makes it worth our while to call distinctly to mind to-day, that primal principle of the Pilgrims, which secured such fruits; and what was that? It was *individualism;*—freedom of the individual conscience and opinion,—the right of private judgment, without the dictation of Pope, bishop, priest, or king. And what did this involve? Plainly the necessity of individual culture, the necessity of education for each and for all. These two ideas, —individual freedom, and individual elevation, were not separated either in their theory or their practice. No sooner had they erected the walls of their dwellings, than they began to lay the foundations of the school house and the church. Education and Religon went hand in hand. In their esteem,—and all our history affirms the same,—these are the guardians of society, the safeguards of the State. In their far-sighted wisdom they perceived the need of something beyond the common school, and so, early in their history, though in weakness and in great poverty, —as we read, they "thought upon a college." There is nothing in the early history of our land more heroic, more touching in its story, than the record of the faith evinced and the sacrifices made in founding the colleges of New England. We thank God that their spirit did not die with them. Beloit College is as truly a child of New England Puritanism as though its walls were standing on Plymouth Rock. It breathes the same spirit, and it has the same aim that characterized the early colleges. It has inherited not only their spirit, but also, what that is sure to secure, a share in their sacrifices. As did their fathers before them, the "poor wise men," of this new western colony have toiled and prayed, giving of their best strength, and their scanty means to build up a college "*for Christ* and the Church," and tho' often weary, never discouraged ; though often hindered, never faltering, until, as surely we may now justly claim, some fruits worthy of their faith and of their effort, have been garnered. It could not be otherwise than that a college so founded and built up in prayer, so pervaded from its very beginning, with religious ideas and aims, should ally itself most closely with that work which is the special care of the Christian church. This has ever been manifest here. Though never a theological seminary, it has taken special delight in fostering those influences which tend to fit young men for the ministry and to bring them into it. It has aimed to be distinctly and thoroughly Christian. Here has been recognized as the grand aim of a true college,—the development of a symmetrical manhood, that is, a *Christian* manhood ; that which includes moral strength as well as intellectual vigor,—the power of living the truth as well as expressing the truth. Here the fact has not been concealed that man has a moral nature as well as a mental power, and both must be cultured, or at best, the education is only partial. Intellectually, the effort has not been to flood the mind with facts,—to pile upon it philosophic theories,—to load it down with erudition,—but rather to arm it with the weapons of truth, and to nerve it with power to wield those weapons. Morally, the aim has never been to bind the soul with the fetters of some religious formula ; to make it pronounce the shibboleth of some sect or denomination, nay, but it has been rather, while throwing around it a moral atmosphere ever stimulating and developing, to bring it into communion with those grand truths of matter and of mind,—of science and of revelation, which teach us our true sphere of duty; which kindle the fires of the heroic soul ; which bring us out of self, and plant our feet on this rock,—loyalty to truth, yea *loyalty to Him who is the Truth.* This is the culture which the age imperatively demands !—the culture needed to counteract that sentiment, too popular at this day, which would divorce religion from education; —which, if it only could make a man an intellectual giant, would gladly leave him a moral dwarf. Let it not be forgotten that that institution of learning which ignores the moral part of man, and cares only for the mental, can never do for society, what society imperatively needs to have done ; can never do for the church, what the church must and ever will demand.

The mightiest human agency which the Divine Spirit ever employs on this earth, is mind educated and consecrated to Christ. But how can this agency be secured without just such institutions of learning, pervaded by the Christian spirit, as that planted in this soil ? As Dr. Kirk once said : " There can be no permanent Christian civilization without a thoroughly educated, godly ministry, and there cannot be such a ministry without the Christian college." How else can be met the great, the pressing want of the west, yea the want of the world,—the want of a *thorough liberal, Christian education ?*

For twenty five years Beloit College has been doing what she could to meet this want. The extent and value of her work are

not indicated simply by statistics, showing how many of her sons
have entered the Christian ministry, for her influence has pervaded every department of activity ; but since I speak particularly
of her relation to the work of Christian evangelization, let me
give you a few facts proving how true the aim of the college has
been to the religious design of her founders.   From the first the
prayer-meeting has held an honored place among her means of
securing a pervading religious atmosphere.   Some of us well remember how, a score of years ago, each Tuesday and Saturday
night a little praying circle met, sometimes in a chamber above,
and sometimes in the chapel below ; and how, even then, the College Missionary Society had begun to turn our thoughts toward
personal effort for both home and foreign evangelization,—organ-
izing us for the Sabbath School labor in the outlying country
districts.   Not a single year has passed without evidence of the
Divine Spirit's special presence among the students; not a year
without the commitment on the part of some of them to a religious life.   The influence of one of those years, 1857–8, when was
organized "The Beloit College Christian Union,"—whether now
felt within these college halls or not, is still abiding, as it ever
will abide, with many of the graduates.   It is a remarkable fact,
I doubt whether it can be paralleled in the history of any other
college, at least in the west, that including those now studying
theology, considerably more than one third,—more precisely—
about forty-two one-hundredths of all the graduates have turned
toward the Christian ministry.   This includes the whole of two
classes, the single graduate of '52, and the nine graduates of '59.
Of these, eight, including one congressman, two or three doctors,
two editors and two connected with colleges, have left the active
ministry for other vocations.   Six have become foreign missionaries, and four have died.   This does not at all include those
who left the college without completing the full course, but who
yet found their way into the ministry, and are honoring the college and the Master by their sincere devotion to it.   One of
these, (Wells,) after faithfully serving and suffering for his country in the time of her need, became a missionary to India, where
he is now toiling.   Another, (Harrison,) whose earnest Christian
spirit the class of 1858 will not soon forget, chose a peculiarly
self denying work, and is honored as the " church building mis-

sionary" on the frontier,—having himself, while preaching, aided with his own hands in erecting some thirteen different edifices ; and now he is bravely leading a colony to a new pioneer work in Nebraska. Another, (Johnson,) of the same class, in the first half of its course, after preaching several years in Illinois and California, entered the editorial corps and is now on the Pacific slope doing manly service for the right. Such,—and there are many others like them,—should now have special mention, be-because not being among the graduates, they might not other-wise be reckoned, as they really ought to be, among those who are adding to the fruits of the college in the work of the world's evangelization.

Of the Alumni who have entered the ministry and who are scattered throughout the Union, and some of them in foreign lands, time forbids my speaking except in the briefest general re-ference. From the oldest graduate,—honored among his minis-terial brethren in this State,—to the youngest who has been com-missioned to preach the gospel, they are a band of laborers that any college in the land might rejoice to send into the vineyard of the Lord. Their labors have not been fruitless. Our Alma Mater may well, with gratitude, recognize the work which the Kind Father of us all has permitted them to do. But especially may she rejoice in her relation through her sons, to the work of foreign missions. The last has been a notable year in her history, and she may with profound gratitude record the fact that with-in the past twelve months she has been permitted to send into the foreign field more sons than any other two colleges in the land. Surely Beloit College has not been founded in vain.

What, through the efforts of her sons, the college has accom-plished in the cause of education in general, has been closely al-lied to,—indeed a part of her work in behalf of the cause of Christ. The interests of religion and of education are in perfect harmony, and the culture of mind and the culture of heart ought never to be separated. Reforms in the church spring from edu-cated men, as the examples of Huss and Wickliffe and Luther and Calvin testify. Long ago Luther said truly, "It is a grave and serious thing affecting the kingdom of Christ and all the world, that we apply ourselves to the work of aiding and instructing the young." History teaches no lesson more plainly than this, that whosoever would control the religion of a people, must control their education. In Austria, at one time, the proportion of Papists to Protestants was one to twenty-nine, and for years, one writer affirms, "scarcely a man could be found to enter the priesthood;" but in one generation she was lost to the Reformation and regained to the Papal hierarchy. And how was this done? By permitting the Jesuits to obtain a controlling influence in the universities. So, too, was it in Poland. In the sixteenth century the Polish diet was essentially Protestant, protected Protestants, printed Protestant works ; but in an evil hour a Protestant king appointed a Jesuit "Minister of Instruction." He filled the professors' chairs with Jesuits, and soon the scale was turned. In the same way the Jesuits recovered to the Papacy the larger part of Europe when it seemed lost to them forever. At one time they had nearly six hundred colleges under their control. They were not so much a preaching order, as a teaching order, and by educating minds they have governed communities and nations. Such facts as these are worth a whole volume of rhetoric. The sons of Beloit College have not been blind to the importance of popular education, nor backward in their efforts to promote it ; nor have they neglected the claims of higher education. Our Alumni are represented by two of their number in the Faculty of their own Alma Mater; by two also in the State University at Madison. One is in the State Normal School at Whitewater. Others are in four different state institutions for the deaf and dumb;—one in Wisconsin, one in Illinois, one in Michigan and one in Louisiana. Two are in medical faculties in Chicago, and two are connected with colleges in other states, while seven others give their profession as that of the teacher. One, now a member of Congress, organized for Alabama after the war, her system of public education. Another, who was expected on this occasion to present more fully the relation of the college to education in general, was for six years State Superintendent of Public Instruction for Kansas, and now worthily stands at the head of Washburn College at Topeka. Another, (Alley,) is bravely leading off in a new college enterprise for Nebraska. In his earnest enthusiasm he says, "If I can do a little

towards putting an educational institution on a solid Christian basis, the embodiment of a living, active faith, to be a power for
truth and good, I will lift up my hands and heart and soul to
God with profound gratitude." Has not this the genuine ring
of Puritan gold? May we not confidently affirm that God's blessing will abide upon him?

But I may not further particularize. As we look back over
the past, and abroad over the field now held, we can but recognize the fact, and rejoice together in view of it, that during these
twenty-five years there has been wrought a work not only for
the social welfare of men, but for the honor of God in the exten-
sion of Christ's Kingdom in the earth. Let these friends of
Christian learning who have toiled and counseled together for
these years gone by, gratefully thank God for what has been
achieved, and with increased faith and earnest zeal, go forward
to the work yet before them, ever looking upward, as in days
past, for the Divine guidance and blessing, assured that with
these, the fruits already garnered shall be but the beginning of
a harvest,—to be gathered as the generations come and pass
away,—which shall ever be increasing in the abundance and rich-
ness of its fruits, until the reapers are done, and seed time and harvest shall be no more.

[In place of the paper from W. A. Montgomery, Esq., Professor Emerson has furnished the following.]

A PAPER:

The Relation of the College to the State.

This theme was assigned to Captain W. A. Montgomery, of the class of 1857. Unexpected and imperious business prevent ed his presenting a subject, which he had already illustrated by able and faithful service, both as a soldier and as a barrister. The topic, however, is so essential both to the duty and to the history of the college, that it cannot be wholly omitted.

While the college is intended to be a religious and literary institution, its object is not merely to educate clergymen, or men of letters. Many of the Alumni are in the medical or legal profession. Some are legislators. A considerable number are editors; the same disposition, which has sustained the College Monthly until it has completed its eighteenth volume and is second in age only to the Yale Literary, has brought the sons of the college into leading connection with journals of sectional and national as well as local influence. The same disposition which has sustained the College Monthly, until it has completed its eighteenth volume and is second in age only to the Yale Literary Magazine, has brought the sons of the college into connection with leading journals in the centres of influence in the State, the northwest and the whole land. Neither should we forget those who, in unprofessional life, are illustrating the value of culture united with the practical activities of life.

The college would have been very untrue to the convictions on which it was founded, and would have studied and taught the lessons of the past to little purpose, if itself or its sons had been indifferent to the great public events which have marked its time. Those events have had a powerful influence upon the education of the young men who have been here; and the college itself has contributed its quota to the great, perhaps the decisive, influence of the American college system in the struggle which has made liberty the law of the Republic.

The college began at the moment when the question of human right became the leading question in the nation. The strife opened in Kansas; and while it was in doubt, the sons of Beloit were there with voice, vote, and rifle: and when that was past, one of them was called to organize the system of public education for the State, and now presides over her Puritan College, while others are in positions of influence in conducting her destinies.

When the war spread across the land, the sons of Beloit, both at the college and elsewhere, answered the call. Of perhaps seven hundred and fifty who could bear arms, we have the names of more than four hundred who were in the field, and of forty-six who died in the service. Probably full reports would give more than five hundred soldiers, and more than fifty who gave their lives. They were good men; more than half of those who lived were made officers; more than half of those who died, died from wounds. As their service was in devotion to the principles which are the soul of the manhood which the college aims to train, it has been fitly recognized by the erection in their honor of a "Memorial Hall," which, on the twenty-fifth anniversary of the college, was made complete by the tablet containing the roll of martyrs. It now stands as an educator for their successors. The enthusiasms of the time were so in accord with the spirit of the college that they could hardly be said to have interrupted its work. Its instructions found rather enforcement than distraction in the events passing without, and its order went right on without interruption, except that one commencement was omitted because the graduates, with the professor of Rhetoric, were in camp at Memphis. As each call came, men went to the field, and when their service was over they returned to the college, not demoralized, but with a developed manhood, which invigorated and ennobled the whole life of the institution. The year of return, 1865, is marked by the commencement of the daily prayer meeting, which has from that time been, not only the heart of the religious life, but a most important influence in all the life of the college, securing harmony, order, study and general health and truth and growth. The same character prepared them to do good service to the country after the war. One was called to organize education in Alabama, and now represents its capital district in Congress;

while others, by teaching and other good work, are securing the results for which their brothers died.

The military record of the college illustrates its relation to all the land. Its sons were found in the regiments of nineteen states, and in nineteen states or territories they died for the common country, and for what they esteemed the common cause of mankind. In coming time, may the nation always be true to humanity and to truth and may the college, in that cause, always be true to the country.

A PAPER:

On the Bearing of College Culture upon Professional Life.

BY H. P. MERRIMAN, M. D.

Of the Class of 1862.

Only two weeks since, did I receive the president's request to prepare a paper for the present occasion: consequently my thoughts have been put together very hurriedly in the uncertain intervals I could command.

The subject he gave me differs slightly from the one announced in the circular. As I received it, it reads thus: "The bearing of the college culture upon the after professional life of the student."

At the time of the first world's fair in London, critics said that the only thing in which America surpassed all other nations was in the "rugged utility" of the articles she presented. This seems a marked American characteristic. We demand the useful in all our institutions, and I believe American ideas would have long since abandoned colleges altogether but for their exceeding usefulness.

Now and then a man is endowed by nature to such an unusual degree that he grasps the foremost place in any profession as an inherent right, because he possesses naturally not only the faculties but the ability to use them, which the average man has to develop and strengthen by a process of education. These are the men we call great. I can imagine Hercules at the Olympic games an easy conqueror in all the trials of strength without undergoing a previous course of training to harden the muscles and to increase the endurance; and in our own time a Lincoln, untutored by the schools, steps easily to the foremost place as lawyer and statesman, a recognized leader of the nation. As there was only one Hercules, so these Herculean men are rare and the value of training is not lessened because a few are strong without it. It benefits these more than the others, for they have more to build upon. It is doubtful if education gives any new faculties,—it gives not powers but *power*.

The object of college culture as I understand it, is to develop and strengthen the powers of the student and teach him their use, thus making him a successful competitor of the man still better endowed by nature but without the training.

Disciplining the mind has always been to me a very indefinite expression. It can perhaps be analyzed with advantage. Probably every one can see how habits of industry and perseverance may be the result of the college discipline and how mathematics may teach close thinking and exact reasoning. Upon these two points I shall say nothing. The third point in the analysis is:

1. The college properly teaches a young man *to be a good learner.*

The *thorough investigation* of one subject,—it makes little difference what one is chosen,—does more to form a habit of thoroughness and accuracy of inquiry, and to teach a man *how to learn for himself*, than many times the study upon subjects which he leaves unfinished.

This is a valuable point to make. The young man who can take up a subject, be it in law, politics or religion, in science, history or medicine;—like, for example, the cause of the present supremacy of Prussia, or, the successes and failures of Louis Napoleon,—or, the prospects of Roman Catholicism in this country—the young man, I say, who can take up any such subject and carry it in mind for months, elucidating one difficulty after another, as his reading or his thought throws more light upon it, until at last he feels that he is master of it,—has gained a power that will be invaluable to him in any profession. Every one is aware of the decided advantage a person has in learning a new language, who has already mastered one besides his own. This is because the faculties used in the study of language become trained, and not necessarily because of any close similarity between the two, for they may differ as much as possible. So the power gained by thoroughly investigating one subject, enables a student to grasp others and diverse ones successfully. In professional life a man must become his own teacher in whatever department of work his lot may fall,—he has to choose his own subjects and the best methods of mastering them. The untrained mind is bewildered under such circumstances, and looks one way and another, seeking some escape and becomes very ready to lean upon any help that may appear. How important then that he should learn how to do this work before necessity compelled immediate grappling with a subject in which his interests were vital. When the need comes thus suddenly upon one all unprepared he may attempt the work that lies before him but the result will be crude and imperfect, a state of things which (however unimportant in college,) he cannot afford in professional life where vital interests attend his labors. Such experiments are too costly—his early practice should be upon less expensive material.

I remember well the remark of a fellow student who had some six months start of me in professional studies. We had been en gaged separately in the investigation of the same subject and had met to compare results. At the close of our comparison he said, "I wish I had gone through college, it so splendidly helps to *get at things.*

The fourth point in this analysis is, the college teach es to form correct judgments. Throughout life the most incessant occupation for the thinker is the solving of doubts and the determining of probabilities. Every one remembers the story of the Dutch justice who said he never wanted to hear but one side of a case, it was so much easier to decide then. We are all a little like this justice, it is easy for us to determine when the evidence is all on one side. Mathematical *certainties* are pleasant to deal in. but the certainties of life are few. In all the professions and in every avocation we shall find ourselves surrounded by *un*certainties which we must face, consider carefully and decide. We must determine, for example, from the great mass of conflicting opinion what we will believe in religion; we must choose which side we will take in the great public questions of the day; which in politics;—whether we will vote for Grant or Greeley; and then momentous questions of duty are continually arising.

The judge on the bench weighing evidence; the physician anxiously combating insidious disease; the general before the battle contemplating its chances; the lawyer at his desk eagerly searching if he can turn the doubtful scale in favor of his client; the merchant calculating the probable changes in gold, grain or goods;—all are balancing uncertainties and settling doubts. To teach a young man to thus carefully discriminate between various doubtful points and to come to correct conclusions, I should not exercise him in mathematics, nor in any of the exact sciences, which deal in certainties and give absolute proof, (I should expect such studies rather to weaken him in this direction,—for when one is taken from a realm of absolute knowledge into one of uncertainties, he feels lost;) neither would I put him directly into his profession, where he could not look coolly—without any self-interest—upon the doubts that arise thick about him. Thus situated he would be in danger of two things,—of becoming one sided, unbalanced, a partisan, if a strong mind: and if not strong, of making a complete failure. Scylla or Charybdis! Few escape.

The course I *should* adopt would be one where from neutral ground, with no self-interest to bias him, he should be the judge trying cases, commencing with easy ones. The classical and literary part of the college course supplies this need more perfectly than any thing else I can conceive of. First in the dead languages to decide the probable meaning of the author in every sentence; yes, to decide the best meaning for every word. When familiar with these, then the Socratic thoughts—the dealings with the sophists. The various questions in history—in logic, determining major and minor premises: besides these discussions and preparation of papers, metaphysics, moral and social science, *all* afford a progressive drill in weighing probabilities and deciding uncertainties.

We come then naturally to the following conclusion: That the college cultivates (a) habits of industry and perseverance. In many instances where students of medicine have attracted the attention of my associates and myself to their earnest working power, we have been pleased to learn that they were college graduates. It is in that way a young man *should* show that he has cultivated powers. Some have erred in thinking their college course would save the necessity of continuous exertion in their professional studies. This is a grand *mistake.* This course is not intended to prepare for *ease,* but for efficient work.

The college cultivates, (b) Habits of close and exact reasoning. (c) The faculty of investigation, teaching how to be a good learner. (d) A correct judgment upon the various affairs of life. These are the faculties most requisite in every profession.

In addition to these acquirements there is a certain variety of accomplishments gained in college, which prove valuable accesories in professional life, a few of which only will I mention. Some aesthetic culture ; a degree of literary polish ; a certain knowledge of Latin and Greek. The little I knew, made our medical vocabulary come very easy to me,—no slight help I assure you, for it enabled me to understand lectures from the very first. In this connection I may add that Dr. Crosby, chancellor of New York University, says that a new word learned is a new idea even though it differ but slightly from those already known. A rich fund of illustration also can be drawn from the classical and scientific culture of the college, which any public speaker will know how to appreciate. What a rich subject I have : broad and fertile as our own prairies. I can but plow a little furrow.

Thus much for colleges in general, but they differ in particulars. There is a noticeable tendency on the part of students educated abroad—whether foreigners or our own countrymen,—to allow authority to take the place of independent thought. " The Professor said so," is with them an ultimatum. We see it continually in the practice of medicine, and for this reason even learned German physicians rarely hold their own by the side of ours, although they require a seven years' course of study against our three. These doctors continually inquire what do the books say this disease is ; or how would my old professor treat this affection ? Imitation is a characteristic of European thought more than of American, though I was recently informed that an eminent professor at Yale announced himself as there to give instruction and not to answer questions. Dr. Lyman Beecher used to encourage his sons in discussion with himself and would rejoice when they had the best of the argument. Such training helped to make the Beechers what they are. And such training is what many of us remember to have received in these halls. May it be long before intelligent inquiry is repressed at Beloit College.

A PAPER:
On the Future of the College.
BY PROF. J. J. BLAISDELL.

The centre of that large and generous outlook, which caused the fathers of the college to be so earnest in giving it being, was the great moral conflict to be waged in these regions. They had entered the northwest as champions of the Christian struggle, and knowing, as all good men know, their own insufficiency and that they must soon leave the field, they had it in their thought to found here an institution for preparing men who should be masters of mind in whatever of the occupations—the ministry especially—there should be occasion for in the growing life of society. Men for Christian service, with no lack of physical fitness and intellectual training, especially brought to truth and strength of character—something of this description was the burden of the prayers and purposes in which the college originated.

Here then, presumptively at least, must be found an answer to any inquiry respecting the Future of the college. Inconsistent is it ever with the continuity of any organic structure, whether institution or human being, to alter the fundamental principle of its life. If you make the change, as indeed you may, it is a revolution so profound as to wrench the future away from the past, and, as at that moment a new life begins, you must call the new structure by another name.

Perhaps, however, from suspicion of failure adequately to accomplish such result may arise a thought that possibly the college had better receive another aim. May it not be wise to omit in part the downrightness of its Christian policy, and by losing something of its explicitness save something of its life. In the twenty-five years now closing, besides the very much larger number who have received its less measurable influence, the college has graduated 175 young men ; of these, in the last seven years, 86. Of these 175, it is not known that all of them have

not been true and effective in bringing into the control of society those general principles which condition its welfare. Many
of them have been in circumstances where they have met the
pressure of heavy onset, have carried themselves with great
steadfastness in behalf of truth, and have largely contributed,
sometimes with their lives, to its triumphs. Out of these 175
graduates of the college, 135 have been avowedly Christian men,
and have gone into the field with the purpose of identifying
themselves with the interests of the highest truth. Of these
many are doing service in other professions, while seventy are
ministers of the gospel, and seven are already engaged in the
work of Foreign Missions. Certainly if it be desirable to be less
explicit as a Christian school hereafter, it must be for other reasons than because satisfactory results have not attended the policy hitherto pursued.

But if not for lack of real success, perhaps for other reasons it
may be thought best to shape the policy of the institution more
nearly into conformity with general systems of education. In
short, will you make it less a school for training young men to
do telling Christian work? Will you cease to make Aeschylus
and Plato a point of departure for opening up to the young the
Desired of all nations? There are some plausible reasons for
this. There is a prevailing drift towards the neutralizing of these
Christian features. In certain circumstances it would ensure
greater ostensible results. It would certainly disarm some preju-
dices. The change is not without noteworthy examples.

Here then, perhaps, is the most fitting place to say, that, according to the view taken by those who administer the college,
in this distinctively Christian work the college has its essential
significancy and value. Take out of the legend on its seal, "*Sci-
entia vera cum fide pura*," the last three words, and the college
drops out of the peculiar desirableness of its mission and ceases
to answer the profoundest wants of this great West.

Far be it from any of us to place a low estimate upon the public system of instruction, which, proceeding upon a compromise
of religious preferences, leaves to other agencies the office of religious instruction. But is it not of the alphabet of the responsibility of Christian men and women, that the youth whom they

can influence should have their mental culture wrought out upon the revealed Christ as its informing principle, and that this cannot be done but by Christian teachers in Christian schools? How without a supply of men thus forged, can the truth be brought into effective operation in society? And has not the history of society taught this at least to those who medicine its ills, that without the inworking of Christ there can be for society no ultimate recovery? What other inference do we reach than this that there must be Christian colleges—colleges which are Christian—to furnish Christian workers?

The conclusion in regard to our future is plain. We must remain a Christian school. As such we must look to the friends of human good for pecuniary support and patronage. They must cherish it, defend it, furnish to it their sons. When you sent your sons to the war of liberty, it touched you to the quick if you found that they were wanting for bread or arms or opportunity. *You have sent this college to the front; maintain it in the condition of effective battle.*

There is no ambition concerning the college which would at length recast it in the form of a university, in which instruction should be furnished for the several professions. So vast are the changes to take place in the coming hundred years of the Mississippi Valley, that, no alteration of this kind is too great to be within the range of possibility. But certainly no demands at present existing furnish occasion for extending the collegiate basis or directing energy to other objects.

The same principle suggests also what must be the policy of the institution in regard to allowing the student freedom in the selection of his studies. Our humble and unpretending work is to take into our midst youth unacquainted with themselves and their ultimate tastes and fitness, and by protracted trial evolve their latent forces and proportions of intellect feeling and will, until, we knowing them and they knowing themselves, they are qualified to choose intelligently what they had better study and what do. There are two distinct periods in life, the period of youth and the period of manhood, the law of the first being ignorance of self, that of the second self knowledge. It has been and is the belief of the college that when a young man really knows what studies he had better pursue, the time has come for him to receive his diploma.

Perhaps it may be from a pardonable enthusiasm in pursuing the single object chosen at the outset that the college has failed to feel the force of reasons urged for combining the sexes in collegiate life. To train young men for service was the problem the administrators of the college assumed. It has seemed to them inclusive enough, noble enough, difficult enough, to task their utmost energies. The measure of success granted them has reinforced the belief in them that their work was legitimate and good.

Be it understood we share in no antagonism with institutions which pursue the policy mentioned. We honor the men who conduct them as brothers in the one good work. Perhaps the experiment may serve for good results. It is likely that for a certain kind of educational culture it may pass into a permanent policy. But for us, assuredly it would widen the work of the college and so make it less concentrated. It would complicate the work if it would be discriminating. If it complicates the work, it makes equal success more costly and doubtful. If it be not discriminating and individualizing, it is of far less value. Certainly it leaves—there is nothing in it so imperative as not to leave—room for narrower and more concentrated work according to our original conception. With a heart therefore open to the efforts of all who make careful experiments in a different direc- we may probably forecast the future of the college as not differing in the particular in question essentially from its past.

But we must not forget that a chief feature of the future of the institution must be the continuance and perfecting of the *relations* which existed in the beginning. A body of instructors furnish the mould of a policy and stand ready to apply the processes by which young minds are formed. But the good men and women of Wisconsin, Illinois and New England, by supplying the needed pecuniary means, by sending hither their sons and inducing others to send theirs, by pouring in upon the college the flood of their sympathy and by the mighty ministry of prayer have filled the mould of that policy and have put under these waiting processes the material. Need we say that such embosomment of the college in the faith of the churches must be the main element of any future we contemplate. In respect to the past alumni of the college at least we are secure. It is not a thing to be feared that they will ever lose their interest in the mother who cherished them. The tokens of their affection are too many to admit of this. The faces we meet to-day and their answers to our salutations confirm our confidence. We hasten to assure ourselves that it will be the same with all: that with those who support the college and with us who administer it, the future may be one of confidence, of affection, of mutual intercourse, of interpenetrating life. With a future such as this, a work mightier than we dream of to-day will be our final record.

The other of the two features that must determine the desired efficiency of the college is, that there be present to do the work of education men possessed of highest personal attainment, intellectual and moral, in the organic form of character; men of the first excellence in science and literature, abundantly gifted with the ability of engaging, quickening and guiding the young; such teachers receiving out of their homes numerous youth, and by their own mighty life evoking all the latent powers of good within them; the fathers of many sons, bearing the family likeness—sons of God.

Such is our view concerning the future of Beloit College. By the steady application of forces already committed to the enterprise, the present number of students tripled or quadrupled, these subjected to all the methods of the most vigorous and complete collegiate culture, moving about amid the multiplying monuments of a pure art, and all the excellent beauties of nature, especially where virtue has her memorials and living exemplars, with the Spirit of God continually brooding over them, growing deep and strong and patient in the presence of great truths, learning at length what they themselves are, their weakness, their strength, their destiny and their duty—and then going out by classes of fifty, year by year, into the field which is the world, to do what God wishes them to do—in the ministry, in the law, in the place of sickness and pain, in literature and art, by the press, in mechanics, in agriculture, in statesmanship—such a future we contemplate. Of such a future we already have an earnest. Such a future seems almost in our grasp. The age needs it for us. God wishes it. Each one, true to his responsibility, we shall have it.

A PAPER:

The Mutual Relations Between the Colleges and the Churches.

BY REV. LYMAN WHITING, D. D.,

Of Janesville, Wis.

Mr. President: The *terms* in the title of the argument you have assigned to me, go far in making the plea which ought to be made, in this closing commemorative utterance. The "*mutual* obligations,"—may I term them?—are either, a great assumption, or a great concession, as between the colleges and the churches. Do the churches and the colleges confess the relations? Does not our national history demonstrate that these "relations" have been *vitalities* between them, and so the "relations" have become *obligations?* Permit me so to call them, the "mutual obligations," as a definition of their "relations." Now mutual obligations have this peculiarity ; viz., a power of mutual enforcement resides along with the obligation; for neither claimant can expect anything, until he has rendered something; because that which he renders, is the foundation of the means to give that which he claims; and so, if either one gives nothing, no right inheres to claim anything. So then the relation or obligation which is "mutual," puts colleges and churches upon the same footing; both claimants upon each other; and to the same extent, both debtors to each other. As these relations are moral, they come at once into line with the glorious governmental plan of the ever-blessed God. It is briefly this : *getting good, is always to come by doing good.* This underlies the whole moral plan of God for this world. Getting, inseparably fastens to doing,—when good is the coupler. Never can real good be gotten, unless real good is done ; and in blessed converse, never is real good done, but as real a good goes from it to the doer. No act with a good issue to one alone is possible, to the actor alone, or to the receiver of the action, alone. Reciprocity overspreads, infuses with perpetual and inevitable commixture, the realm of moral acts. That business or scheme, giving good or profit to one person or

party only (and such there are,) is a nefarious, an inevitably per-
nicious thing. (e. g. the liquor traffic in this country; thuggery
in India; great and rapid gain to the dealers; hideous death to
the victims.) That supreme good act of the moral universe,—
Jesus Christ's atonement,—has in it infinite reciprocity; infinite
glory to the Godhead, and eternal glory to the redeemed. One
measures the other.

So the colleges,—this preeminently, as a child of the churches,
—gets as it gives, and gives as it gets, good from them. Trace it.
The churches first do the royal good work of founding it,—
giving it an existence,—a location; a body through which to live,
move and have its being. Out of its very first class goes back
to the churches, a prepared gift of piety and of culture, worth
alone all costs up to this time, and which reminds one of the
mustard-seed, with branches for the birds, and seed-pods for re-
producing itself athwart the globe. Each soul that has been, or
shall be led to Christ in that life-time, is a return gift to the churches
for their service in giving the college an existence. Out of each
of the twenty-one other companies of educated youth, this church-
planted college has bestowed upon the world, have been gifts to
the churches of pastoral service for which we have no scale of es-
timation. What is one regenerated soul worth—even in this
world,—when it reproduces itself by the conversion of others, and
they in turn repeat their divine birth in growing numbers, and
these in ever swelling progression multiply the "sons of God,"
until the final expansions are millions of regenerated souls, and
all the boundless benefits of their Christian life to every good
thing in society and the world, can be accredited to the one new-
born soul, in whom began the process   Try the estimate upon
such college converts as Whitefield, the Wesleys, Jonathan Ed-
wards, Henry Martyn, Gordon Hall and hundreds like them, who.
if in less eminence, in no less distinctness, have begun careers in
college, which have made them to be like stars in the firmament.
Out of this college how many have already gone just like them
in spirit and in heroic labors? To visit them all, you must liter-
ally circumnavigate this globe. To calculate their worth to the
world, you need the computations of eternity. But first the
churches *gave* the means, and the sons to be educated. That giving must have been done, or the college could have returned no

such inestimable recompenses. Only as the churches bestow means and men upon the college, can the college give back this grand propagating, mental and spiritual manhood upon the churches. Dry up either spring, and both streams are gone. Churches never have lived and grown, without pastors ; and pastors have never been found of any great use to the churches, unless there were schools to train and fit them for their work. The schools have commonly found the best material in the churches, and often out of the most unpromising stock, has schooling fashioned the most powerful and valuable servants of the church.

You all have heard of,—some here have seen,—Mt. Athos, the stately bulb of the Actean promontory, flinging its huge shadow for leagues, 'tis said, across the hills of Lemnos on one side, and over the Ægean's waves, on the other. When Alexander the Great, wore the Persian and Median empires as his crown, and the waves of his shining victories irradiated the outmost shores of the known world ; a poetic architect named Stasicrates, proposed,—as an embodiment of the demigod men thought the conqueror to be,—to carve this Mt. Athos into a magnificent statue of Alexander, six thousand feet high, holding in its left hand a city of ten thousand inhabitants, and pouring through a horn of plenty in its right hand, a copious river into the sea at its feet !

Was a more insane magnificence ever proposed ? What a master-piece of workmanship ; what an exaltation of human genius ; and what a majestic flattery that completed, would have been ! But this college has done and waits to do, grander sculpture than that had been. It takes the rugged, shapeless bulbs of young manhood and carves them into " temples," such as the Holy Ghost dwells in ; into better than statues,—living men, "full of faith and of the Holy Ghost," and in place of a river from classic cornucopia, the " water of life springing up into eternal life," flows through them to dying myriads.

Such work this college,—all Christian colleges,—have done, are still doing, and, if the churches will quarry the marbles, provide for and maintain the sculptors here at work, such will be the products to the end of time.

Colleges and churches in *mutual relations!* Yes: together they rise; they stand together, and together, if ever—they will fall. Neither can exist alone, and each doing good to the other, gets a greater good to itself, and either sowing sparingly for the other, will also reap sparingly from it; but as God is true, and as all history testifies,—each sowing bountifully to the other, shall reap *more* bountifully that it has sown.

FINIS.

APPENDIX.

A

THE FINANCIAL DEVELOPMENT.

At this stage in the history of the college, a brief and summary statement of the sources from which the funds for its support and endowment have been drawn and of its financial condition seems appropriate.

Agreeably to, and indeed, beyond their first pledge, the citizens of Beloit donated ten acres of land for a site and contributed about $8,000.00 for the erection of the first building. The site has been, by subsequent purchases, doubled so that it now embraces over twenty acres.

The first donation from any one outside of Beloit was in 1845, the gift of 160 acres of land by Rev. Henry Barber of Dutchess Co., N. Y. This was given at the suggestion of Rev. S. Peet, through whose agency, this with other lands in Wisconsin, had been saved to the absent owner. A condition was attached to the gift that the college should open its doors to students without distinction of race or color. The land was sold for $1,000.00 and the avails appropriated to the enlargement of the site. There being, at the time, no other source of income, the trustees contributed from their own pockets to meet the taxes and expenses of sale.

The first foundation for a professorship was laid by Hon. T. W. Williams of New London, Conn., in 1847. On a visit to his relative, Mrs. Peet, he became interested in the college enterprise and gave lands lying in Wisconsin and Indiana which yielded nearly $10,000.00. By subsequent donations of Mr. Williams, this fund has been increased to $12,000.00.

The nucleus of a library was gathered in 1848, chiefly by contributions of books made by eastern friends to Prof. Bushnell, who, at the same time, secured the Saybrook scholarship of $500.00, the first provision for the relief of indigent students. To this the Austin scholarship of $500.00 was added in 1850, through the agency of Rev. A. Kent.

In 1849, Rev. David Root, then of Connecticut, began his contributions towards endowing a second professorship, by transferring lands and claims in the West. The whole amount brought into the treasury, after a course of years, from this source is $10,000.00, held on a condition similar to that of Mr. Barber's gift.

In that year also, Rev. S. Peet as agent, commenced canvassing the West for means to meet the current expenses. His efforts, at length, brought in something over $8,000.00, nearly one-half of which was contributed by ministers, on this missionary field, out of their scanty salaries. Friends in Milwaukee showed their good will for the college and for their pastor, called to be its president, by the gift of $2,300.00 to the permanent funds. Soon after, Prof. Bushnell collected in Chicago $3300.00 additional for permanent investment.

In 1850, Rev. M. P. Squier pledged for the endowment of the chair of Mental and Moral Philosophy to which he had been elected, the sum of $10,000.00. The pledge was, at a later date, redeemed by the transfer of property and claims which have realized the full sum.

In the autumn of the same year, the largest donation from any one person was made by Mrs. Sarah W. Hale of Newburyport, Mass., in the form of deeds for over five thousand acres of land in Illinois. The avails of this generous gift have amounted to $35,-C00.00, of which $25,000.00 are set apart as an endowment for the chair of mathematics and the remainder was, with the consent of the donor, applied to sustain the life of the college in the crisis of the late war.

In 1854, Rev. Dr. H. N. Brinsmade of Beloit, began his contributions towards endowing the Latin Professorship for which he has already paid into the treasury $7,000.00, with the expressed purpose to add to it hereafter according to his means. During the same year, the education fund for the aid of needy students was raised to $4,000.00 by a bequest of $2,000.00 from Joseph Otis, Esq., of Norwich, Conn., and $1,000.00 from Capt. John Emerson and his heirs.

The large endowments came in a form such that some time was requisite to convert them and make them productive. Meanwhile, current expenses must be provided for. During eight successive years beginning with 1849, the College Society from its collections in the east, made annual appropriations for this purpose, which averaged $1,000.00 per annum. During the years 1853–4, Rev. S. O. Powell, Rev. H. Lyman and the president were successively engaged in special agencies to secure similar relief from the West. The avails of these efforts, coming in through a series of years.

amounted to $15,000.00. For three years from 1858 to 1860, aid was received from the Regents of the state normal fund, on account of students preparing to be teachers, which amounted in the aggregate to $3,300.00. These resources, with some incidental contributions from other quarters have sustained the operations of the institution, for the most part without debt or detriment to permanent endowments.

In 1857, the bequest of Mrs. L. Colton of Beloit, whose watchful regard for the college had been manifested, from time to time, in gifts for specific objects to the amount of $1,000.00, secured a permanent fund of $5,000.00 for the increase of the library. In the year 1866, the name of Rev. Dr. Ralph Emerson was also identified with the library through gifts from members of his family of property, whose avails will ultimately amount to not less than $15,000. In the year 1854-5, a building for the accommodation of students was erected at an expense of $7,000.00, which was met by a temporary loan, subsequently paid up from funds received for general purposes. In 1858, the citizens of Beloit made a special contribution of $3,000.00 for the erection of the chapel. Three-fifths of the cost of the building was thus provided for.

In the year 1863, were commenced special efforts to strengthen the foundations of the college financially, by agencies in both the West and the East. Rev. P. C. Pettibone undertook this service in the West. The burden of labor in the East devolved on the President, under the auspices of the College Society. The effort in the East, in connection with the results of previous, partial agencies, realized the sum of $30,000.00 to be added to permanent endowments. In this amount are included a gift of $10,000.00 from an anonymous friend, one of $5,000.00 from Winthrop S. Gilman, Esq., of New York, and many other generous contributions ranging from $50.00 to $1,000.00 each. Mr. Pettibone's service, continued for nearly seven years, yielded good fruit in the addition of some $60,-000.00 to the resources. This includes $12,000.00, the avails of property donated by O. Harwood, Esq., of Wauwatosa, to endow a professorship, $1,500.00 realized from the bequest of Miss Nye of Falmouth, Mass., and nearly $18,000.00 collected from hundreds of alumni and friends all over this region, for the erection of Memorial Hall. The remainder was given for general purposes, to a considerable extent in the form of scholarships, in accordance with a plan adopted some years before. The books of the college show fifteen permanent scholarships of $500.00 each and one hundred and six individual scholarships of $100.00 each, fully paid. Partial payments in other cases, swell the whole amount contributed in this form to $20,000.00. This plan has been a means of increasing the number of students as well as the resources, with no serious embarrassment. It is however, deemed advisable hereafter to suspend issuing individual scholarships, except as pledges have been already given.

Among the miscellaneous donations which have come from unlooked for sources to meet various exigencies, the gifts of $500.00 from Miss Elizabeth Davis of Boston, as a fund for the purchase of books on English literature and of $500.00 from Mrs. Ripley of Chicago, as a fund for providing chemicals &c., for the scientific department, deserve a mention as those most recently received.

This review of the financial development of the college brings freshly to mind the struggles and trials through which its growth has been made. At the same time, it gives occasion for devout gratitude to Almighty God, whose favor has so richly blessed the enterprise and for hearty thanks to the many friends whose timely benefactions have been divinely ordered to meet the ever expanding wants of the institution.

The present resources of the college are exhibited in the following concise statement:

PERMANENT FUNDS.

1. Professorships:	Williams Professorship,		$12,000.00		
	Hale	do	25,000.00		
	Squier	do	10,000.00		
	Root	do	10,000.00		
	Brinsmade	do	7,000.00		
	Harwood	do	12,000.00	76,000.00	
2. Endowments not designated,		-	-	-	30,000.00
3. Education Funds,	-	-	-	-	9,000.00
4. Library Funds,	-	-	-	-	15,000.00
5. Prize Funds,	-	-	-	-	600.00

Total invested funds, $130,600.00

UNPRODUCTIVE PROPERTY.

1. Site and Buildings,	-	-	-	75,000.00
2. Library, Cabinet and Apparatus,		20,000.00		95,000.00

Total property of the college, $225,600.00

The current expenses of the college exceed the certain income by from $2,000.00 to $3,000.00 each year. The deficiency has been thus far met by miscellaneous subscriptions and the sale of scattered pieces of land. This resource is nearly exhausted. Only one of the professorships is more than half endowed. Meantime, there is urgent pressure for the enlargement of the work involving an increased scale of expenditure. Such enlargement seems imperatively necessary to put the college forward in the future, as its prestige in the past warrants and demands.

Means are now urgently needed

To increase endowments for the Department of Instruction,

To provide for the care of the Library,

To equip the Scientific Department,

To give a distinct establishment to the Preparatory School,

To improve the Grounds and Buildings,

To increase the Fund for aiding worthy young men,

To provide a Gymnasium, and

To secure a reliable income for Miscellaneous expenses,

Under the pressure of these wants, and with a view to the enlargement of the college that it may keep pace with the rapid development of the great Interior in which it stands, the Trus'ees are constrained to invite a general co-operation of those who appreciate its importance in an immediate effort to raise the sum of $200,-000.00 to be added to present resources. Shall they ask in vain ?

B.

THE FEMALE SEMINARY.

In estimating the results of the plan instituted by the conventions which established Beloit College, we should take into view also the Female Seminary, which was an essential part of the same design. Originating with the same conventions, and committed at first to the same trustees, it was finally located at Rockford, Illinois, in 1850, and has since been carrying on its work parallel with that of the college. With a view to the best efficiency of each, the Boards of Trustees have become somewhat distinct in their membership, as they are in their legal relations; but they still represent the same sympathies, and the results of the two institutions belong to the history of the common plan.

The seminary occupies a site of about twelve acres on the eastern bluffs of Rock River, within the city of Rockford, and yet retired as well as healthful and beautiful. It has accommodations for two hundred boarders, as well as for the various requirements of a comprehensive course in literature, science and the fine arts. Its collegiate course, like that of the college, extends through four years. There are also preparatory and normal courses, each of two years, as well as excellent facilities for instruction in music and other accomplishments.

The first Principal, Miss Anna P. Sill, is still at the head of the school, supported by twelve competent teachers.

It has sent forth nineteen classes, and two hundred and thirty-nine graduates, two hundred and one from the full course and thirty-eight from the normal course. More than three thousand pupils have been within its walls.

As the result of the religious influence continually present in the institution, it is estimated that not less than five or si x hundred of its pupils have been converted there; and of the two hundred and one full graduates one hundred and ninety-one, and of the thirty-eight normal graduates thirty-two went forth as Christians. Fifteen of the former teachers or pupils have become foreign missionaries, while those who remain at home are doing their part toward the Christian culture of the land.

If the seminary did not, like the college, send four hundred sons to the war, it was a centre of that living and efficient sympathy, by which American women sustained and comforted those who went. Its daughters also were found among those whose labors in teaching secured the results of the work of war.

The seminary is now doing its work, with a fair provision as regards accommodations, and some of the materiel of instruction. It needs endowments; and it needs the continuance and the continual renewal of the enlightened and Ch ristian sympathy and co-operation in which it originated, and by which it has thus far been cherished.

THE AGGREGATE RESULTS.

It will have been observed that the movement in which Beloit college originated, contemplated the co-operation of the friends of Christian liberal education, especially of Congregationalists and Presbyterians, in the section lying between Lake Michigan and the Mississippi, in building a college and a female seminary. Theological education has, as was natural, been provided by the several denominations at Chicago, the commercial focus of the region, —leaving the college and the seminary to pursue, in the heart of the country, their specific work, upon the common basis of evangelic truth and sound learning.

We have, then, as the results of the movement, two institutions, essentially collegiate in their character, one in sympathy and differing in location, administration and courses of study, with a view to the highest efficiency of each in forming intelligent and Christian manhood and womanhood. Each presents a collegiate course of four years, supplied by a preparatory and supplemented by a shorter course. Both have now been at work for a period of from twenty to twenty-five years. Nearly five thousand pupils have been, for a longer or shorter time, connected with them, and are now diffusing their education as well in the thousand homes, as in the colleges, schools and churches, public journals, legislative bodies, or courts of justice and other public positions, in which they preside or act. The young men from the college who have preached the gospel in more than twenty of our own states or territories, and the former members of both institutions, who have gone to many foreign peoples, illustrate the wide scope of the influence, which goes from such centres to all the world and in all honorable occupations. Four or five hundred are now in them year by year; they come from and go to all the world.

More than four hundred have completed the full courses of instruction, and, both by the positions which they fill in the world and by the manner in which they fill them, are confirming the persuasion of the value of such a training, which lay at the root of the whole design.

How have the two institutions realized the hopes of their founders in their religious influence? It has been the continual effort in each to present the fear of the Lord as the beginning of wisdom and the vital knowledge of God as the consummation of education. It is to be thankfully recorded that scarcely a year, or even a term, has passed in either without conversions. It is estimated, that not less than eight or nine hundred have embraced the Christian hope during their course. Of four hundred and twenty-seven graduates, more than three hundred and fifty were professors of religion.

Beside those who are engaged in Christian work in all sections of our land or in Canada and England, twenty-five of their former members have gone on foreign missions, to stations almost encircling the globe—to the Dacotah and the Creek Indians, the Sandwich Islands and Micronesia, to Japan and China, to Burmah and Hindoostan, to Egypt and Turkey, and home by the West Indies and the American Indians who still remain in our eastern states. These results of the period of infancy may encourage the hope and prayer that the two institutions may, in their maturity, do their part toward the salvation of the world.

ERRATA.

On page 4th, line 16th, instead of "Now," read *For*.

" " 10th, " 4th, " " "their," " *these*.

" " 11th, transpose the first two lines of Mr. Clary's paper.

" " 29th, line 3d, instead of "have ever," read *elsewhere*.

" " 37th, lines 15th to 18th inclusive are superfluous.

" " 48th, line 22d, instead of "Desired," read Desire.

www.ingramcontent.com/pod-product-compliance
Lightning Source LLC
Chambersburg PA
CBHW021522090426

42739CB00007B/742